NATIONAL GEOGRAPHIC

D0602852

WORLD EXPLORERS

African Journeys

1850–1900

Danny Miller

PICTURE CREDITS
Cover (back), pages 1, 2, 3 (top), 4 (top right), 24 (top right), 31 Pitt Rivers Museum, University of Oxford; cover Robert Harding Picture Library; pages 3, 10, 28–29, 30 (top and bottom) Mary Evans Picture Library; page 4 (bottom) Hulton Archive/Getty Images; page 5 (bottom left) Museum of Mankind, London, UK/Bridgeman Art Library; page 5 (middle), 7 (top) Royal Geographical Society Picture Library; page 5 (bottom right) National Geographic/Getty Images; page 6, 14 Corbis; page 7 (bottom right) Science & Society Picture Library; pages 8 (top), 11 (bottom) Kennan Ward/Corbis; pages 8 (bottom), 13 (left), 15, 20 (right) Hulton-Deutsch Collection/Corbis; pages 9 (left), 16 (bottom left), 20 (left), 22, 23 Bettmann/Corbis; page 12 Chinch Gryniewicz/Ecoscene/Corbis; page 13 (right) Nik Wheeler/Corbis; page 16 (top left) Stephen Frink/Corbis; page 16 (bottom right) Patrick Ward/Corbis; pages 18–19 Royalty-Free/Corbis; pages 19 (top), 22 (bottom), 27 (left) DK Images; page 21 Werner Forman/Art Resource, NY; page 24 (top left) John Conrad/Corbis; page 24 (bottom) Liverpool Record Office, Liverpool Libraries; page 26 Bill Gentile/Corbis; page 27 (right) Jonathan Blair/Corbis; page 29 (top left) British Museum, London, UK/Bridgeman Art Library; page 29 (right) Durand Patrick/Corbis Sygma.

Produced through the worldwide resources of the National Geographic Society, John M. Fahey, Jr., President and Chief Executive Officer; Gilbert M. Grosvenor, Chairman of the Board; Nina D. Hoffman, Executive Vice President and President, Books and Education Publishing Group.

PREPARED BY NATIONAL GEOGRAPHIC SCHOOL PUBLISHING
Ericka Markman, Senior Vice President and President, Children's Books and Education Publishing Group; Steve Mico, Vice President, Editorial Director; Marianne Hiland, Executive Editor; Anita Schwartz, Project Editor; Jim Hiscott, Design Manager; Kristin Hanneman, Illustrations Manager; Diana Bourdrez, Picture Editor; Matt Wascavage, Manager of Publishing Services; Sean Philpotts, Production Manager.

MANUFACTURING AND QUALITY MANAGEMENT
Christopher A. Liedel, Chief Financial Officer; Phillip L. Schlosser, Director; Clifton M. Brown, Manager.

ART DIRECTION Dan Banks, Project Design Company

CONSULTANT/REVIEWER
Dr. Margit E. McGuire, School of Education, Seattle University, Seattle, Washington

BOOK DEVELOPMENT Nieman Inc.

BOOK DESIGN Three Communication Design, LLC

PICTURE EDITING AND MANAGEMENT
Corrine L. Brock
In the Lupe, Inc.

MAP DEVELOPMENT AND PRODUCTION Elizabeth Wolf

Published by the National Geographic Society
1145 17th Street, N.W.
Washington, D.C. 20036-4688

ISBN: 0-7922-4545-8

Printed in Canada

cover: hippopotamus attacking David Livingstone's boat
back cover: brass fish; **page 1:** mask; **page 2:** musical instrument; **page 3 (top):** covered bowl shaped like antelope head; all objects collected by Mary Kingsley in Africa
page 3 (bottom): David Livingstone and African porters

Table of Contents

Africa in 1850

By 1850, European explorers had traveled over much of the world. Their maps showed far fewer unexplored areas. However, much of Africa was still unknown to people outside of it. Europeans wanted to know more about this vast area—its geography, natural resources, and people.

Europeans wanted Africa's wealth, such as ivory and gold. They wanted to sell Europe's goods to the Africans. European **missionaries** wanted to teach African people about Christianity and to work for their welfare.

◀ Crocodile mask

Explorers had long tried to reach central Africa, but getting there was difficult and dangerous. Dense jungles covered much of the area. The wildlife could be deadly. There were tiny insects whose bites carried disease. Huge hippos might overturn an explorer's boat. The people there sometimes attacked outsiders.

Between 1850 and 1900, several explorers traveled from England into Africa. Their reasons for going were very different.

Richard Burton and John Speke wanted to become famous for finding the **source** of the Nile, the place where Africa's greatest river begins. David Livingstone was a missionary who wanted to end the African slave trade. Henry Stanley was a journalist who went on a rescue mission to find Livingstone. Mary Kingsley wanted to learn about the animals and people of Africa. These explorers had different goals, but they were alike in their courage and strength in facing hardships.

◀ Lion attacking explorer
David Livingstone

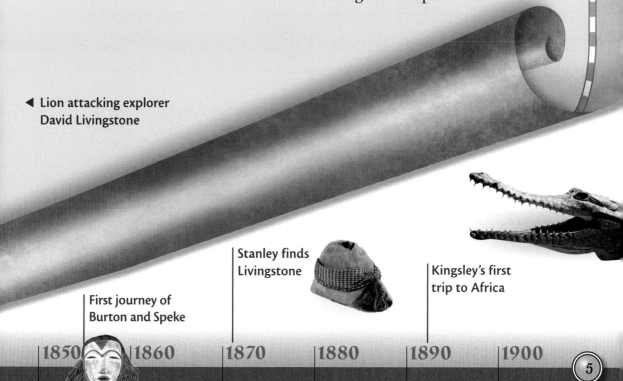

Stanley finds
Livingstone

Kingsley's first
trip to Africa

First journey of
Burton and Speke

1850 1860 1870 1880 1890 1900

In the 1800s, explorers in Africa could travel by land or by water. If they traveled by land, they most likely went on foot. Their journeys lasted many months. So, explorers needed to take a lot of supplies and equipment. This gear included tents, food, clothing, guns and ammunition, scientific instruments, and medical supplies.

All this gear had to be carried great distances over difficult country. So, one of the first things an explorer had to do was to hire a lot of Africans to serve as **porters** to carry the expedition's supplies. Explorers also needed guides, cooks, and people who knew African languages.

African porters carry explorers' gear.

Some men aboard Livingstone's steamboat fire at an elephant on the Zambezi River in southern Africa.

Africa has many great rivers, and some explorers chose to travel by water. David Livingstone used a paddle-wheeled steamboat to explore rivers in southern Africa. Mary Kingsley learned to paddle an African dugout canoe. Travel by water was faster, but it had its problems too. On many African rivers, **rapids** and waterfalls made it impossible to use steamboats.

Paddling a dugout could be risky too. Mary Kingsley found this out when a crocodile tried to crawl aboard!

African travelers needed to bring a ▶ supply of medicines.

Chapter 1

Burton and Speke

Richard Burton was an officer in the English army. He came from a wealthy family and had always longed to explore faraway lands. Burton was well educated and knew many languages. He could speak Arabic very well. He was able to avoid being caught when he dressed in Arab clothing and made a trip to Mecca. Mecca is a holy city for **Muslims**, believers in Islam, the religion founded by Muhammad. Burton's trip was very dangerous. Non-Muslims were not permitted in Mecca, and he might have been killed.

In 1854, Burton decided to travel into Africa. He asked three other English officers to join him, including John Speke (speek).

Burton and Speke were unlikely partners. Burton was very outspoken, and Speke was shy. Burton liked books, and Speke liked hunting. But both wanted to become famous explorers.

Richard Burton

AFRICA

Nile River

Kilometers
0   500   1000
Miles
0   500   1000

N
W   E
S

A F R I C A

Equator

Lake
Victoria

Ujiji

Tabora

Lake
Tanganyika

INDIAN

ZANZIBAR

OCEAN

◀ John Speke

Burton, Speke, and their companions started their trip at a village on the east coast of Africa. One night, people from the area attacked them. One of the four was killed. Burton received a spear thrust in the face that scarred him for life. Speke was captured, but managed to escape.

This was the end of their first attempt to journey into Africa. They returned to England, and Burton wrote about their experiences in a book. Speke was angry that Burton didn't give him credit for showing much courage in the attack.

A Miserable Trip

By 1856, Burton had a new goal. He wanted to be the first explorer to find the source of the Nile River. Burton had heard rumors of an "inland sea" somewhere in central Africa. Could this be where the mighty river began? Although the two explorers were no longer friendly, Burton asked Speke to help him on this new journey. Eager to return to Africa, Speke agreed to come along.

The explorers began their journey inland from Zanzibar, a group of islands off the east coast of Africa. It took them over four months to reach the village of Tabora. It was a miserable trip. Many of the Africans with them gave up and left the caravan. Burton and Speke both became very ill with **malaria**, a dangerous tropical disease. At one point, Speke was so sick he lost his eyesight for a time.

Burton travels on a donkey across Africa.

Finally, on February 13, 1858, the two men reached the top of a hill. Burton saw what they had been searching for. There below him was a great inland sea. It was Lake Tanganyika (tan–guhn–YEE–kuh), the longest freshwater lake in the world. Speke's temporary blindness robbed him of his first sight of Lake Tanganyika. He later wrote, "From the summit of the eastern horn, the lovely Tanganyika Lake could be seen in all its glory by everyone but me."

◀ Zanzibar was an important trading center in the 1800s.

Boats on Lake Tanganyika today are like those Burton and Speke saw.

The Quarrel

The caravan made its way down to Ujiji (oo-JEE-jee), a village on the shore of the lake. Burton and Speke heard stories about a river at the north end of the lake. If the water flowed out of Lake Tanganyika and into the river, perhaps they had found the source of the Nile. The explorers tried to reach the north end of the huge lake in canoes.

They were still very ill and had to turn back. Burton believed that they had discovered the source of the Nile, but Speke had his doubts.

Back in Tabora, the two kept arguing. Speke asked if he could make a trip on his own to check out a rumor that there was another large lake to the north. Burton finally agreed, as he later admitted, "to get rid of him."

On August 25, 1858, Speke found the other lake. He was soon sure that this second lake was the true source of the Nile. Speke named it Lake Victoria, after the queen of England, and returned to Tabora to tell Burton the good news. Burton was not happy to hear Speke's claim.

Burton reading ▼

Burton wanted to be the one to solve this great mystery. He told Speke he was wrong. Burton was sure that Lake Tanganyika was the true source.

Speke wanted to return to Lake Victoria with Burton to prove his case. But Burton was still sick, and the two men were almost out of supplies. Speke decided to return to England alone. He promised that he would wait for Burton to reach London before he shared any of their discoveries.

The Nile River

Triumph and Tragedy

Two days after arriving in England, Speke broke his promise to Burton. He made a speech at the Royal Geographical Society and announced that Lake Victoria was the source of the Nile. Speke was treated like a hero. The government decided to send him back to Africa without Burton to further explore the area.

When Burton returned to London two weeks later, he was furious. For the next year, he wrote articles and books attacking Speke. Richard Burton's once promising career now seemed to be over. John Speke had the attention of the world.

Speke reporting his discovery in London

On Speke's next African journey, he and another explorer James Grant, returned to Lake Victoria. On July 28, 1862, Speke came to the spot where Lake Victoria flowed out into a great river. He began to travel north on the river. But Speke was again very ill and low on supplies. He had to give up. When Speke returned home, he declared once more that he had found the Nile's source.

Richard Burton went on the attack. He said that Speke had not proven anything. Since he did not follow the river out of Lake Victoria, he couldn't be sure that this was the source of the Nile. Finally, the men decided to settle the matter in a public debate.

In September 1864, on the day before the debate was to take place, John Speke died in a mysterious shooting accident. He was, however, later proved right. Lake Victoria is the source of the Nile.

Was Speke's Death an Accident?

Speke was reported to have shot himself by accident with his own gun. He was an experienced hunter who had handled guns all his life. Because of this, there remains a question about whether Speke's death was truly an accident. Some people have suggested this shy man simply did not want to face the debate with Burton.

Chapter 2

Stanley and Livingstone

✤

David Livingstone was born to a religious family. As a boy, he loved to wander around the countryside collecting plants and rocks. Livingstone wanted to become a missionary and bring his religion and love of adventure to the unexplored lands of Africa.

Dr. Livingstone's first trip to Africa was very difficult, but he loved every minute of it. He learned as much as he could about the cruel slave trade. Livingstone hoped his writings about the slave trade would help to put an end to it.

Victoria Falls

David Livingstone

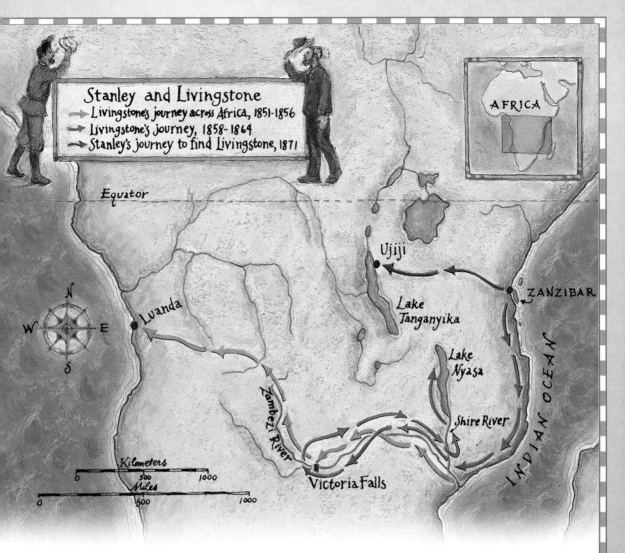

Stanley and Livingstone
→ Livingstone's journey across Africa, 1851-1856
→ Livingstone's journey, 1858-1864
→ Stanley's journey to find Livingstone, 1871

AFRICA

Equator

Ujiji

ZANZIBAR

Lake Tanganyika

Lake Nyasa

Luanda

N
W   E
S

Zambezi River

Shire River

INDIAN OCEAN

Kilometers
0   500   1000
Miles
0   500   1000

Victoria Falls

In 1851, Livingstone traveled up the Zambezi River and came to the edge of a huge waterfall. The crashing waters made a deafening sound and sent a cloud of spray high into the air. The local people called the falls *Mosi-oa-Tunya,* or "The Smoke That Thunders." Livingstone named them Victoria Falls in honor of his country's queen.

Between 1853 and 1856, Livingstone became the first European to travel all the way across Africa. It was an amazing accomplishment. He returned to England a national hero. He wrote a popular book and traveled around the country giving lectures. All the time, Livingstone longed to return to his beloved Africa.

Farther into Central Africa

On his next trip to Africa, Livingstone searched for a good route for future missionaries to take into central Africa. He first tried the Zambezi River. His trip up the Zambezi was a nightmare. He was always surrounded by mosquitoes. The boat got stuck in the mud and damaged by rocks. Many of the men Livingstone hired got malaria and almost died.

Livingstone gave up on the Zambezi and tried another river, the Shire. After traveling hundred of miles past dangerous rapids, he came to the shores of Lake Nyasa (nee-AH-sah), the second largest lake in Africa. The people who lived nearby greeted Livingstone with poisoned arrows. He soon learned the reason for their anger and fear. This was one of the places where Arab slave traders came to capture slaves.

Sunrise over Lake Nyasa

Livingstone and his crew on the Shire
River near Lake Nyasa

During the course of his difficult journey, most of the men with Livingstone died or left the group. One man left with all of the medicine. Livingstone had no way to send news back home and was convinced that the people there had forgotten about him. Several English newspapers had even reported that Livingstone was dead. Soon people around the world asked the same question— where was the famous explorer?

The Story of the Century

James Gordon Bennett, the owner of the *New York Herald*, was looking for a big story to sell newspapers. He decided to send Henry Stanley, one of his best reporters, to search for David Livingstone. Stanley was a talented journalist who also loved adventure. Bennett's order to "Find Livingstone!" was Stanley's most exciting assignment. He didn't know how he was going to locate the missing explorer. He did know that this could be the story of the century!

Stanley arrived in Zanzibar in January 1871. He heard a rumor that a white man had been seen in Ujiji two years earlier, near the shore of Lake Tanganyika. That sounded like a good place to begin his search.

Henry Stanley with an African servant ▶

Stanley (second from left) looking at a map

This tale is a fable, a story meant to teach a lesson. It presents an African view of how Europeans gained power in Africa. The man is meant to stand for the Africans. The elephant is meant to stand for the Europeans.

Once upon a time, an elephant made a friendship with a man. One day, a heavy thunderstorm broke out. The elephant went to his friend, who had a little hut at the edge of the forest.

The elephant said, "My dear good man, will you please let me put my trunk inside your hut to keep it out of this heavy rain?" The man, seeing the fix his friend was in, agreed. He said, "My dear good elephant, my hut is very small, but there is room for your trunk and myself. Please put your trunk in gently."

As soon as the elephant put his trunk inside the hut, he slowly pushed his head inside. Finally, he flung the man out in the rain, and then lay down comfortably inside his friend's hut.

The elephant said, "My dear good friend, your skin is harder than mine, and as there is not enough room for both of us, you can afford to remain in the rain while I am protecting my delicate skin from the hail storm."

African wood carving of a Swedish ▶ missionary reading a book

Stanley on his journey

How I Found Livingstone

✤

In November 1871, after walking more than 1,000 miles (1,610 kilometers), Stanley arrived in Ujiji. He put on his best white suit and had his men fire their guns into the air. A crowd of Africans came out of the village and gathered around the reporter.

Suddenly, Stanley saw a tall, elderly white man walking towards him. The man looked very tired and walked with a limp. Stanley stared in disbelief. Could it be? As the man got closer, Stanley greeted him, "Dr. Livingstone, I presume?"

Livingstone's compass

It was Livingstone, who was so grateful to see someone from home that tears came to his eyes. Stanley stayed with him for four months exploring the area around Lake Tanganyika. The two men became close friends.

Stanley begged Livingstone to return to England with him, but Livingstone refused. He still had work to do in Africa.

Back home, Stanley wrote about his experiences in a book called *How I Found Livingstone in Central Africa*. In 1873, Dr. Livingstone died in Africa. His body was sent back to England. Huge crowds attended his funeral in London. Henry Stanley led the funeral procession and helped carry his friend's coffin.

Stanley meeting Livingstone at Ujiji

Chapter 3

Mary Kingsley

African brass fan

Mary Kingsley had a very unhappy childhood. Her father was a doctor who traveled a lot. Mary's mother was often ill and had to stay in bed much of the time. Mary was left to do most of the work in the house and had no time to play or make friends. Any money for school went to her younger brother, Charles.

Mary taught herself to read. She spent every spare moment in her father's library reading books about explorers and travels to distant lands. It was her only escape. Girls didn't have a lot of opportunity to travel in the late 1800s. Mary was too busy caring for her family to even consider leaving home.

Mary Kingsley

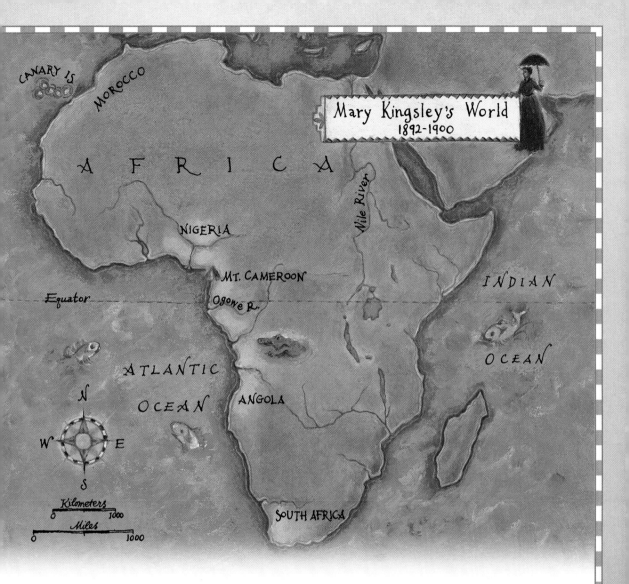

CANARY IS

MOROCCO

AFRICA

Mary Kingsley's World
1892-1900

Nile River

NIGERIA

MT. CAMEROON

Ogowe R.

INDIAN

Equator

ATLANTIC

OCEAN

OCEAN

N

W   E

S

ANGOLA

Kilometers
0   1000
Miles
0   1000

SOUTH AFRICA

In 1892, when Mary Kingsley was 30 years old, both of her parents died. Kingsley still had to look after her brother. When he left England, she could finally follow her dream to travel. Her first trip was to the Canary Islands, off the coast of Africa. Kingsley loved everything about the trip.

She visited a volcano, camped out in the open air, and did things that were very unusual for a woman traveling back then. Kingsley heard stories about people canoeing from village to village, trading with the local tribes for food and shelter. No European woman had ever traveled to West Africa. She wanted to be the first.

First Trip to Africa

At first, everyone thought Kingsley was crazy for wanting to travel into the heart of Africa. Many men had died making this journey, but Kingsley could not be talked out of her trip. She collected goods that she could bring on her trip to trade with Africans. Even those who thought she was risking her life began to admire the determined woman.

On her first trip in 1893, Kingsley explored the west coast of Africa from Angola to what is now Nigeria. She got along well with the African people. As she traveled to villages away from the coast, Kingsley was often the first European these people had ever seen.

A West African village today

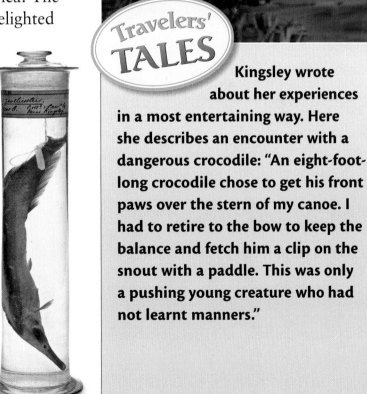

Kingsley didn't believe in traveling just for fun. She had two important goals. She planned to collect samples of different kinds of fish to give to the British Museum. She also wanted to study the religious beliefs and objects of the different tribes.

After her first trip, Mary Kingsley found life in England very dull. She longed to return to the adventure of Africa. The British Museum was delighted with the specimens of fish that Kingsley brought back. They wanted her to travel to other parts of Africa to find other **species**. A species is a scientific grouping of related living things.

West African fish collected by Mary Kingsley ▶

Travelers' TALES

Kingsley wrote about her experiences in a most entertaining way. Here she describes an encounter with a dangerous crocodile: "An eight-foot-long crocodile chose to get his front paws over the stern of my canoe. I had to retire to the bow to keep the balance and fetch him a clip on the snout with a paddle. This was only a pushing young creature who had not learnt manners."

Meeting the Fang

Mary Kingsley began her second trip in Nigeria. Her goal was the large and unexplored Ogowe (oh–goh–WAY) River. She wanted to look for fish there and study a people called the Fang. Little was known about the Fang. There were rumors that they were **cannibals**, people who eat human flesh.

The trip was long and difficult, but Kingsley found her way to the Ogowe and a Fang village. One night, while staying at a Fang house, Kingsley noticed a terrible smell coming from a bag hanging from the ceiling. She looked inside and was shocked to find a human hand, four eyes, two ears, and some toes! Kingsley didn't stay too much longer in the Fang village.

Kingsley (seated left of flag) on the Ogowe

Fang wood mask

After a year in Africa, Kingsley decided to climb Mount Cameroon, the tallest peak in western Africa. Again, everyone thought she was crazy. The explorer insisted that she could make the dangerous trek up the mountain. It was a struggle, but she became the first European woman to do so.

When Kingsley returned to London in 1895, she became famous writing books and speaking about her adventures. As always, she longed to leave England to continue her travels. In 1900, Kingsley went to South Africa to work as a nurse. She caught a fever there and died. Kingsley's work helped give the world a whole new picture of Africa and its people.

Mount Cameroon

Africa in 1900

These explorers added greatly to the outside world's knowledge of African peoples and cultures. This had some good effects. David Livingstone helped end the slave trade in Africa. Mary Kingsley wanted outsiders to respect African peoples and their beliefs. Her writings did not present Africans as less civilized than Europeans. Kingsley felt strongly that other countries should only trade with the Africans, not try to change them.

There were bad effects too. European countries soon carved up most of Africa into **colonies**. A colony is an area ruled by another country.

French and German officials agree on the boundary between their African colonies. ▶

Although these outsiders brought some good things to Africa, they also brought misery and hardship to its peoples. Europe's colonies in Africa would not become independent again for many years.

Glossary

✦

cannibal a person who eats human flesh

colony an area ruled by another country

malaria a dangerous tropical disease transmitted by the bite of a type of mosquito

missionary a person who travels to another place to teach the people there about a religion and to work for their welfare

Muslims believers in Islam, the religion founded by Mohammad

porter a person who carries baggage

rapids a part of a river where the water flows very quickly, often over rocks

source a place where a river begins

species a scientific grouping of related living things

Sculpture that Mary Kingsley brought back from her first trip to Africa ▶

Index